German Halftracks
in Action

Captions Kurt Rieger

Squadron/Signal Publications

Photocredit:

Bundesarchiv Koblenz
Hanz Zarbst
Egon Bloom
Archiv Squadron/Signal
Uwe Feist Archiv
Walter J. Spielberger Collection
Kurt Rieger

NSU Kettenkrad 'HK 101' (Sd.Kfz.2)

In 1940, the NSU Werke AG in Neckarsulm received an order from the **Heereswaffen-amt** to develop a light prime mover to be specifically used by mountain troops.

An O-series of 500 vehicles was put into production with delivery scheduled from July 1940 until late 1941.

Powered by a 36 h.p. Opel 'Olympia' engine which was located behind the driver's seat, the **Kettenkrad** went into full production in 1942 and by December, 1200 vehicles were delivered to the troops. The automobile manufacturer Stöwer, Stettin, also started production and thus a total of 2450 **Kettenkräder** left the factories in 1943, to be followed by 4490 finished vehicles in the year 1944. Originally intended for towing light mountain guns, mortars, the MG36 and telephone wire drums, the **Kettenkrad** was soon found useful in all branches of the **Wehrmacht**. Its extremely good cross-country ability, being able to overcome obstacles such as the mud-bogged roads of Russia or the rugged terrain of the Caucasus Mountains, made it a favorite with the soldiers on the Eastern Front.

Of a total of 8,345 NSU **Kettenkräder** built during World War II, several hundred vehicles survived the War to find a peaceful use by the agricultural and forestry services in Germany. A well preserved **Sd.Kfz.2** in running condition, can be seen at the **Militär-historische Ausbildungszentrum** (Military Historical Center) of the **Kampftruppenschule I** (**Bundeswehr**) in Hammelburg, Germany.

Technical Data

Producer ...... NSU Werke AG Neckarsulm, Stöwer Werke, Stettin
Crew ....3 men
Weight .... 1.3 t (1280 kg)
Loading Capacity .... 325 kg
Pulling Capacity .... 450 kg
Motor .... 1 x 4 cyl. 1.5 ltr. Opel-Olympia (water cooled)
36 P.S. (H.P.) at 3400 r.p.m.
Speed..Road 70 Km/h
Fuel Capacity .... 2 x 21 ltr. (10 gal.)
Fuel Consumption ....Road 16 ltr/100 km
Cross-country 22 ltr/100 km
Range .... Road 260 km
Cross-country 190 km
Dimensions................. Length: 300 cm
Height: 100 cm
Width: 120 cm
Production .... approx. 8345 vehicles

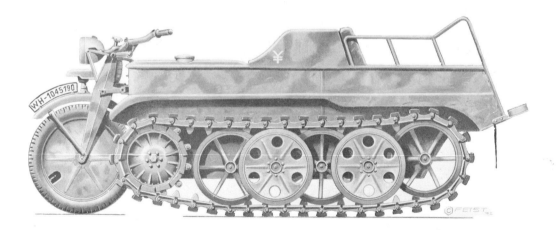

Side view drawing of the NSU 'Kettenkrad' (Sd.Kfz. 2)

The NSU 'Kettenkrad' was an extremely rugged vehicle, able to negotiate the most rugged terrain. A 1.5 ltr. Opel-Olympia engine of 36 h.p. powered this vehicle of which a total of 8345 were built by NSU, Neckarsulm and Stöwer, Stettin. It was also planned to incorporate Simca in the 'Kettenkrad' program.

Retrieving a captured Jeep on the Western Front. The camouflage consists of **Wehrmacht** sand with brown-green mottle.

Designed for a crew of three men, the 1280 kg vehicle could carry a weight of 325 kg and had a pulling capacity of 450 kg.

The 'Maultier' Series

The trucks of the German Army performed satisfactorily during the early campaign against the Western Allies.

A good road network and mild weather conditions gave the supply units of the advancing Panzer Divisions only minor problems such as punctured tires, overheated engines and broken fanbelts. However, this situation changed drastically when the **Wehrmacht** launched a gigantic assault not only against a mighty army, but into a country which would demand more of a mechanized army than the Germans could then imagine.

The offensive against the Red Army in 1941 was well planned and a total of approximately 70,000 trucks and half-tracked prime movers were available to supply the advancing armies. All trucks originated from commercial types, and the dusty, bumpy roads of

To increase the cross-country ability of the production trucks in Russia, a running gear was placed under several German **L.K.W.** types of the **S-Ausfuhrung**, namely the 3t Opel-Blitz, the 3t Magirus, the 3t Ford V8 shown in the photo on the left and the 4.5t Mercedes-Benz.

Russia soon took their toll. In the winter of 1941-42, the **Wehrmacht** faced its first crisis when thousands of vehicles hopelessly bogged down in the muddy and icy terrain of the Russian tundra. Unable to move under their own power, they had to be abandoned.

Since the majority of the supply vehicles of the **Wehrmacht** consisted of the 3t **LKW** of the 'Schnell Programm' this type was chosen to be improved. A developing project of the **Waffen SS** incorporated the British Carden-Lloyd running gear for the 3t truck. The loading capacity of the vehicles dropped to 2t. Production was started by the truck manufacturing firms of Opel, Ford, Mercedes-Benz and Klöckner-Humboldt-Deutz.

Officially designated **Gleisketten-Lastkraftwagen 2t 'Maultier'** (**Sd.Kfz.4**), Hitler accepted a completion schedule of 1870 units until December 31, 1942.

Opel utilized their 3t Opel-Blitz Type 3.6-36 S for the 'Maultier' production. The 'Maultier' was powered by a 6 cyl. 3.6 ltr. gasoline engine with 68 P.S. at 3000 r.p.m., while Ford converted their 3t V8 type G 398 TS/V 3000 S, a truck which was not very popular with the troops.

The Mercedes-Benz Type L 4500 R, was very reliable and the running gear of the **Pz. II** was fitted under this truck.

The best of the lot, Magirus Type S 3000 by Klöckner-Humboldt-Deutz, was only built in small numbers. Powered by a very reliable 80 P.S. 4 cylinder Diesel engine, the Magirus 'Maultier' pulled through the thick mud where otherwise only fully-tracked vehicles could move.

Almost 22,000 3t 'Maultier' vehicles were produced until 1944 by the three firms, while only 1500 Mercedes-Benz 4.5t 'Maultier' left the production line.

Technical Data

	'Maultier' Opel-Blitz Typ 3.6-36S/SSM	'Maultier' Ford Typ V3000 S/SSM	'Maultier' Magirus Typ S 3000 S/SSM	'Maultier' Mercedes-Benz Typ L 4500 R
Producer:	Opel, Rüsselsheim/Brandenburg	Ford, Köln/Berlin	Klöckner-Humboldt, Deutz/Ulm	Daimler-Benz, Stuttgart, Mannheim
Weight	3.9 t	3.9 t	4.6 t	7.7 t
Loading Capacity	2 t	2 t	2 t	4.5 t
Dimensions:				
Length	600 cm	635 cm	615 cm	786 cm
Height	205 cm	210 cm	280 cm	235 cm
Width	228 cm	225 cm	225 cm	320 cm
Motor	6 cyl. Opel-Blitz 3.6 ltr. 65 P.S. at 3000 r.p.m.	8 cyl. Ford V8 3.9 ltr. 95 P.S. at 3500 r.p.m.	4 cyl. Deutz-Diesel 80 P.S. at 2250 r.p.m.	6 cyl. Daimler-Benz-Diesel 112 P.S. at 2250 r.p.m.
Speed	38 km/h	40 km/h	38 km/h	36 km/h
Fuel Capacity	82 liters	110 liters	70 liters	140 liters
Fuel Consumption:				
Road	50 ltr/100 km	60 ltr/100 km	40 ltr/100 km	40 ltr/100 km
Cross-Country	100 ltr/100 km	120 ltr/100 km	100 ltr/100 km	120 ltr/100 km
Range:				
Road	160 km	180 km	170 km	200 km
Cross-Country	80 km	80 km	80 km	100 km

A Ford Type G398 TS/V3000 S (**Schnell Ausf.**) converted as 'Maultier' of a support unit of the 2. Panzer Division on the Eastern Front. The vehicle was powered by a 95 h.p. 3.9 ltr Ford V8 engine. The Ford truck proved to be the least suitable vehicle of the German trucks to overcome the obstacles of the rough Russian terrain and was not very popular with the troops. The running gear was a copy of the British Carden-Lloyd design.

Raupenschlepper Ost 'RSO'

The 'RSO' Raupenschlepper Ost was a design of the Steyer Werke, Austria. Here, the vehicle is shown pulling a 10.5 cm le.F.H. 18M L/28.

To further improve the mobility of the **Wehrmacht** supply units on the Eastern Front, a fully-tracked truck was developed in 1942 by Steyer, Austria. The **RSO** was not a prime mover, however it was frequently used to pull a light anti-tank gun or howitzer. The vehicle was primarily designed to eventually replace the **Maultier** as a supply vehicle.

Powered by a Steyer V8 gasoline engine of 70 h.p., the **RSO** was very slow with only 20 Km/h and could not keep up with a Panzer Division. A crew of two men found room in the fully enclosed and heated driver's cab, while the Magirus-built **RSO** powered by a 65 h.p. Diesel engine, had a canvas top. Full production of the **RSO** began in 1943 when the following firms were included in the **RSO** production program: Klöckner-Deutz-Magirus, Ulm Gräf und Stift, Wien, Auto Union, Werk Wanderer, Siegmar.

A total of over 27,000 **Raupenschlepper Ost** had been produced by 1945 and these vehicles served well under all weather conditions on the Eastern Front as well as in Italy and Western Europe.

Painted in **Luftwaffe** blue-grey, a **'RSO'** with a 7.5 cm **Pak 97/38** in tow.

In a temporary white camouflage, a **'RSO'** as a supply transport vehicle on the Eastern Front. The ruggedness and reliability of the vehicle made it very popular with the troops.

A total of 27,000 **'RSO'** were produced by Steyer, Magirus, Gräf und Stift and Wanderer.

15 cm Panzerwerfer 42 (Sf.) auf LKW Opel 'Maultier' (Sd.Kfz. 4/1)

To improve the mobility of the **Nebelwerfer** units and to increase the rate of fire of the 15 cm **Werfer** (rocket launcher), three hundred Opel-Blitz **'Maultier'** chassis were converted into light armored mobile rocket launchers.

The ten-barreled 15 cm **Panzerwerfer 42** was mounted on the rear of the armored compartment on a turntable traversing 360° and elevating 45°. The vehicle's weight was 7t and it had a top speed of 25 m.p.h.

15 cm **Panzerwerfer 42 (Sd.Kfz. 4/1) auf Maultier** (Opel). Armed with a ten-barreled self-propelled rocket launcher, it fired the same projectiles as the 15 cm **Nebelwerfer 41.**

The vehicle weighed 7.1t and had a road speed of 25 m.p.h. Maximum range of the 15 cm rockets was 73,000 yards and the HE projectile had a 28 pound bursting charge.

With a crew of four, the **Panzerwerfer 'Maultier'** was a very effective weapon. Ten rounds of rocket projectiles were carried in the vehicle. The secondary armament consisted of a **MG 34** or **MG 42** and a **MP.**

Three hundred Opel-Blitz **'Maultier'** were converted into armored **Panzerwerfer.** The cross-country ability was sufficient despite the overloaded chassis.

The launcher is loaded from within the compartment. The projectile weighed approximately 75 pounds and could be handled by one man. The weapon was fired electrically by a gunner sitting inside the vehicle below the launcher platform. A higher rate of fire could be achieved compared to the unprotected **Nebelwerfer 41**, since the crew could remain near the weapon behind armor and could reload the barrels in less time.

Leichter Zugkraftwagen 1t Typ D7 (Sd.Kfz.10)

A **1t le.Zgkw.** (Prime mover) pulling a **3.7 cm PAK 35** on the Eastern Front. The early version had a different type of driving sprocket, road wheels and idler wheel.

Development of a light 1t prime mover began as early as 1934, when Demag built several protoytpes. However it wasn't until 1937 that a satisfactory vehicle was derived and the 6th series powered by a 90 h.p. 3.8 ltr. 6 cylinder Maybach NL38TRKM engine officially designated **le.Zgkw. 1t Typ D6**, was built in greater numbers and issued to the troops. Mass production of the final version, the **le.Zgkw. 1t Typ D7** began in 1939 and continued throughout the war until 1944. The Firms of Demag, Berlin; Adler, Frankfurt am Main; Bussing-NAG, Braunschweig; Phanomen, Cottbus and Saurer, Wien delivered a grand total of over 25,000 1t chassis of which 7500 were converted into the light **S.P.W. (Sd.Kfz. 250)** (covered in Squadron/Signal Armor No. 2 **'Schutzenpanzerwagen in Action).**

The **Afrika Korps** successfully utilized a great number of the **1t Zgkw**. An anti-tank gun unit wearing goggles to protect their eyes from the penetrating fine desert sand is moving full-speed into action.

Rugged and easy to operate, the **1t Zugmaschine** performed well on all Fronts throughout the War.

Supporting **Panzer IIB** of the **21. Pz.Div.**, a **1t Zgkw.** is seen pulling a **5 cm PAK.**

This very rare picture shows the canvas covered rear compartment of the **1t Zgkw.** with rifle racks on top of the front fenders. Camouflaged in **Wehrmacht** sand with brown-green splotches, this unit is seen operating in the guerilla territory of the Balkans. Note the trooper holding his **MP** at ready.

The low vehicle allowed easy dismounting for the crew. Despite one missing road wheel, the **Zgkw.** remained fully operational.

Panzerjäger with a **5 cm Pak 38.**

(top left) **Luftwaffe Panzergrenadiere** manning the **1t Zgkw.** The vehicle to the right is a **3t le.Zgkw.** (**Sd.Kfz. 11**) of a **Panzerjager** unit towing a 5 cm **PAK 38.**

3.7 cm PAK (Sf.) auf le.Zgkw. 1t, a field conversion to increase the mobility of the anti-tank gun. This vehicle, shown operating in Russia, was built by the Adler Werke, Frankfurt am Main.

Towing a 21 cm **Nebelwerfer 42,** a **le.Zgkw.** of an unidentified unit is moving into position.

2 cm Flak 38 (Sf.) auf le.Zgkw. 1t (Sd.Kfz. 10/4)

The **2 cm Flak 38** mounted on the **le. Zgkw.** weighed 420 kg and had a rate of fire of 480 r.p.m. (practical 220 r.p.m.). The trailer to the right housed additional ammunition.

The net at the right-hand side of the gun would catch the spent cartridges. The magazine can be seen clipped onto the gun opposite the cartridge sack.

Compared to the cold wintery conditions of the Russian Front, this **2 cm Flak** crew obviously appreciates their assignment under the blue skies of Greece. Note the open ammunition box with one 20 round magazine partly visible.

17

The partly armored version of the self-propelled **2 cm Flak 38** on the Eastern Front. The trailer behind the gun carried additional ammunition and the personal belongings of the crew.

Ammunition boxes holding two magazines each are fitted on the outside of the vehicle.

Flak Personnel
(9 Month Service)

A considerable number of the **1t Zgkw.** were converted into anti-aircraft units. The containers on top of the front fenders housed two **Karabiner 98K** each.

A pause during the fighting gave this **Flak** crew a chance to catch up on some long needed sleep. The tally on the gun shield includes two tanks and twenty-eight aircraft!

With a crew of seven men, the **Sd.Kfz. 10/4** could travel at a top speed of 50 km/h. 115 liters of gasoline stored under the driver's seat gave the vehicle a range of 300 km on the road and 170 km cross-country.

On target - - **Russki-Ford Type BA.**

With ammunition magazines stacked high, a **2 cm Flak** unit is seen in action. The **2 cm Flak 38** had a range of 4800 m and an effective ceiling of 3700 m.

Leichter Zugkraftwagen 1t (Sd.Kfz. 11)

The Hansa-Lloyd-Goliath Werke AG, Bremen (1939 Borgward) were charged in 1933 with the development of a prime mover capable of towing loads up to three tons. The first prototype equipped with a 3.5 ltr. 6 cylinder gasoline engine, the 'HL kl 2' was completed in the following year to be replaced by a second prototype of the 'HL kl 3' in 1936, while development of the 'HL kl 5' continued in the same year. Over 500 units of this type were constructed.

Simultaneously a number of prototypes with the engine located at the rear of the vehicle were built for trials with armored superstructures.

In 1938, the development of the half-track prime mover came to a final conclusion with the introduction of the 'HL kl 6'. This version remained in production until November 1944 and was also built under License by Hanomag, Adler Skoda and Wanderer. Approximately 25,000 3t Zgkw. chassis left the production lines of these companies by the end of the War. Of this total amount, 16,000 chassis were converted into the medium armored personnel carrier (m.S.P.W. **Sd.Kfz. 251**).

Technical Data

	Le. Zgkw. 1t Type D6	Le. Zgkw. 1t Type D7
Crew	8 men	8 men
Weight	3.4 t	3.4 t
Dimensions;		
Length	475 cm	475 cm
Height	160 cm	160 cm
Width	193 cm	193 cm
Loading Capacity	1.5 t	1.5 t
Pulling Capacity	1 t	1 t
Motor	6 cyl. Maybach NL 38 TRKM (gasoline) 90 P.S. at 2800 r.p.m.	6 cyl. Maybach HL 42 TRKM (gasoline) 100 P.S. at 2800 r.p.m.
Transmission	7 forward, 3 reverse	Variox SPG
Speed	65 km/h road	65 km/h road
Fuel Capacity	90 liters	90 liters
Fuel Consumption		
Road	38 ltr/100 km	38 ltr/100 km
Cross-Country	65 ltr/100 km	65 ltr/100 km
Range:		
Road	230 km	300 km
Cross-country	230 km	170 km

A **Luftwaffe** 5 cm **Pak** anti-tank gun crew in a blue-gray **le. Zgkw. 3t** prime mover. The chassis of the **3t le. Zgkw.** was also utilized as a basis for the **m.S.P.W. (Sd.Kfz. 251)** developed by Hansa-Lloyd, Bremen. The picture shows the final version of the **3t Sd.Kfz. 11.**

Leichter Zgkw. 3t HL kl 6 (Sd.Kfz. 11)

The chassis of a Borgward type **HL k/6** is undergoing a cross-country test. The 110 ltr. gasoline tank is fitted in the rear part of the frame

Charged in 1933 with the development of a tractor capable of towing loads up to 3 tons, the Hansa-Lloyd-Goliath Werke AG, Bremen, completed a prototype in 1934. The final chassis of the 3t prime mover can be seen here.

The **Afrika Korps** received a number of the 3t prime movers which were mainly used for towing the **10.5 cm leichte Feldhaubitze 18** (105mm light field howitzer 18).

The gun crew, wearing the light tropical helmets, are enjoying the cool breeze on top of their speeding prime mover. This vehicle is the subject of the color drawing on the back cover.

(left) The road to Tilimun Soluoh in the Cirenaica changed hands several times. The British sign indicating the necessity of posting an observer on vehicles driving in this area is evidence of the activity of the **Luftwaffe**.

With a specially designed superstructure to hold 36 rounds of 15 cm **Nebelwerfer 41** projectiles or 10 rounds for the 21 cm launcher, the Hanomag built **le.Zgkw. (Sd.Kfz. 11/5)** carried a crew of six men.

(below) The front end arrangement showing the single transverse leaf spring, two shock absorbers and the forged axle beam. The front wheels were of pressed steel with tires of size 190-18; no brakes were fitted. The vehicle in this picture is a **m.S.P.W.**, the front end arrangement of the 3t **Zgkw.** is identical.

A medium decontamination vehicle (**Sd.Kfz. 11/2**) (**mittlerer Entgiftungswagen**). The vehicles carried approx. 25,000 pounds of bulk decontaminant and a number of hand cannisters of 22 pounds each. A distribution hopper was fitted on the rear of the vehicle. 28/32 cm **schweres Wurfgerat 41** (**Nebelwerfer 41**) are positioned in the background, ready to fire incendiary 32 cm rockets.

78. Infanterie-Div.

Loaded with paratroopers of the **Division 'Hermann Göring'** a **Sd.Kfz. 11** towing a 3.7 cm **Pak 35** anti-tank gun is moving through an Italian town. Summer 1943.

25

1. Infanterie -Div.

A typical scene on the Eastern Front showing supply trucks moving ammunition to the front under the protection of a **Pz.IV Ausf. H**, while a 5 cm anti-tank unit is relocating.

Part of a Panzer Division is pausing on a road in Poland during the early days of the Russian Campaign. All vehicles are painted in dark-gray.

Mittlerer Zugkraftwagen 5t (Sd.Kfz. 6)

Two main versions of the 5t prime mover were built by the Firms of Büssing-NAG and Daimler-Benz. **Sonderkraftfahrzeug 6** was used as a **Pionierfahrzeug** (engineer's vehicle) while **Sd.Kfz. 6/1**, the **Artilleriefahrzeug** (artillery vehicle) served to pull the **le. FH 18** howitzer.

With a crew of 7 men, **Sd.Kfz. 6/2** was a 3.7 cm **Flak 35** self-propelled anti-aircraft vehicle. The total weight of this vehicle being 10.4t, the ammunition for the 3.7 cm was carried in a one axle trailer.

Mittlerer Zugkraftwagen 5t (Sd.Kfz. 6/1) Artillerie Ausführung with a 10.5 cm **le.F.H. 18** (light field howitzer) in tow.

A brand new 5t prime mover, painted in **Wehrmacht** sand color. The troops in this picture are **Gebirgsjäger** (mountain troops) crew of an **8.8 cm Flak 18.**

A very unusual conversion into a **Panzerjäger-Selbstfahrlafette** took place in 1941 when nine 5t prime movers were armed with the Russian 7.62 cm **Pak.** The armor box was installed around the **Pak** by the Altmärkische Kettenfabrik, giving the 10.5t vehicle a very high and clumsy appearance. A small number of these vehicles operated in North Africa, and one was later captured by the British.

A prime mover is being unloaded from a small freighter by members of the **'Deutsches Afrika-Korps'.**

Mittlerer Zugkraftwagen 8t (Sd.Kfz. 7)

The 8t 'Sonderkraftfahrzeug 7' may well be considered the most important and versatile prime mover of the German **Wehrmacht**.

Originally implemented to haul the old 7.5 cm cannon, the 8t Zgkw. (**Sd.Kfz. 7**) acted as a prime mover for the deadly 8.8 cm **Flak**. Many engagements on the Eastern Front or in North Africa were decisively influenced by the '88' made mobile through the **8t Zugmaschine**.

Design work on the '**Sd.Kfz. 7**' can be traced back to 1934 when the Firm of Krauss-Maffei AG. Munchen introduced a medium prime mover **Typ 1934**, powered by a 115 P.S. Maybach gasoline engine. The vehicle, with a weight of 11t and a pulling capacity of 8t, was first built by Krauss-Maffei as '**KM m 8**'. Daimler-Benz and Bussing NAG also produced this vehicle under license, designated '**DB m 8**' (**Daimler-Benz mittlerer 8**), '**BN m 8**' (**Bussing NAG mittlerer 8**).

Running off the production line from 1935 until 1936, the **Typ 'KM m 9'** was a Krauss-Maffei exclusive. These vehicles were intended to tow the **s.F.H. 18, s. 10 cm Kanone 18**, or the 8.8 cm **Flak** respectively. A crew of eleven men found room in the open vehicle which carried a canvas cover and had a collapsible windshield. Except for the 140 P.S. Maybach-HL 62 engine installed in the **Typ 'KM m 10'**, everything remained the same with this new type of which production began in late 1936.

The final version of the '**Sd.Kfz. 7**' series, the '**KM m 11**' having a total weight of 11 tons and built by both Krauss-Maffei and Hansa-Lloyd (Borgward), left the production lines in mid 1939.

A total of over 12,000 '**Sd.Kfz. 7**' (**KM** and **HL**) were built until late 1944 when production finally ceased, making the 8t prime mover the most numerous of all the German **Zugmaschinen** built from 1934 until 1944.

It may be of interest to note that the Italian Firm of Breda built the **Zgkw.** under license. The **'Breda 61'** had right hand steering, a 130 P.S. engine, and differed from the German version only by having a slightly different engine hood. The British Vauxhall Motor Ltd. built six prototypes of the **8t Zgkw.** before the end of World War II.

Rear-view of a **Luftwaffe** 8t prime mover **'KM m 8'** towing the famous 8.8 cm **Flak 18** on **Sonderanhänger** (trailer) **201.**

Technical Data

Mittlerer Zugkraftwagen 8t Typ KM-HL m 11 (Sd.Kfz. 7)

Producer . . . . Krauss-Maffei, Borgward
Crew . . . . .11 men
Weight 9.7t
Dimensions:
                    Length . . . . .685 cm
                    Height . . . . .260 cm
                    Width . . . . .235 cm
Loading Capacity 1.8t
Pulling Capacity 8t
Motor . . . . .1 x 6 cyl. Maybach HL 62 TUK (gasoline) water-cooled
                               140 P.S. at 2600 r.p.m.
Speed. . . . . Road, 50 km/h
Fuel Capacity . . . . 215 liters
Fuel Consumption . . . . Road 80 ltr/100 km
                             Cross-Country 160 ltr/100 km
Range . . . . .Road 250 km
                             Cross-Country 120 km

Luftwaffe-Kraftfahrer (Driver)

Reichswehr maneuver in the Lüneburger Heide, September 1935. Pulling a 15 cm **s.F.H. 18** (heavy field howitzer). the 8t **Zgkw.** represented the first production type from Krauss-Maffei. The '**KM m8**' was built from 1934 until 1935 and was subsequently replaced by the '**KM m9**' in 1935.

The 8t **Zgkw.** '**H.L. m10**' was externally identical to the '**KM m 9**'. A new engine powered the Hansa-Lloyd built '**H.L. m10**'. With a crew of eleven men including the driver, a 15 cm field howitzer unit is moving along a rainy country road in Northern Germany, prior to World War II.

A lengthened running gear and different fenders were the most noticeable external changes of the final production series, Krauss-Maffei 'KM m11'.

The front end arrangement of the 8t Zgkw. prime mover with **Luftwaffe** license plates (**Wehrmacht Luftwaffe**).

The 8t prime mover had a luggage rack on the top rear of the vehicle, primarily to store additional gasoline jerry cans. With the **8.8 cm Flak 18** in tow, a **Flak** outfit of the '**Afrika Korps**' is following the advancing Panzers.

Kraftfahrer (Driver)

Built in large numbers from 1939 onward, the 8t prime mover served throughout the war with the German Army as well as with the **Luftwaffe.**

A **Luftwaffe Flak** unit in North Africa.

To prevent unnecessary usage of the running gear as well as to increase the mobility of the Panzer Divisions, the fully tracked vehicles were often hauled to their new assignments by trailer. An 8t prime mover is shown pulling the self-propelled anti-tank gun **4.7 cm PAK (t) Ausf. B.**

An armored **Flugabwehrmesswagen** (anti-aircraft detection vehicle) **Sd.Kfz. 7/6** with an 8.8 cm **Flak.**

Clad in their heavy overcoats against the early morning chill, a heavy artillery unit is moving into new positions.

The 2 cm quad 38 had a weight of 1.5t and was mounted on the **Lafette 400** as a **Sf.** A high rate of fire (practical 800 r.p.m.) and a range of 3700 m, made this a very effective anti-aircraft gun.

8t Zgkw. (Sf.) 2 cm Flakvierling 38 (Sd.Kfz. 7/1).

Range finder (left), gunner, squad leader (with binoculars) and loader, the crew of a 2 cm **Flakvierling** in action.

The **8t Zgkw. mit 2 cm Flakvierling 38 (Sd.Kfz. 7/1)**, (8 ton semi-tracked tractor with 2 cm quadruple anti-aircraft gun 38). A **Luftwaffe** unit pulling an ammunition trailer (**Sd. Anhänger 56**). The vehicle has a crew of six men and carried an additional 600 rounds of ammunition. Note the rifles fixed on top of the front fenders.

Fully armored late **Sd.Kfz. 7/1** dug in on the Eastern Front.

Sd.Kfz. 7/2 mounting the 3.7 cm **Flak 36** with gunshield and ammunition trailer (**Sd.Anhg. 56**), Russia, summer 1942. This vehicle will be the subject of a color drawing in a future publication.

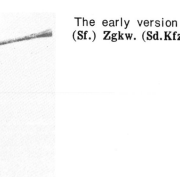

The early version of the **3.7 cm Flak 36 auf 8t (Sf.) Zgkw. (Sd.Kfz. 7/2)** had no gunshield.

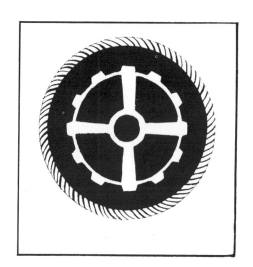

Motor- or Armd Craftsman

The 3.7 cm **Flak 36** had a practical rate of fire of 120 rounds per minute and an effective range of 4800 m. The gun weighed 1.5t.

The late version **Sd.Kfz. 7/2** had an armored cap and radiator, here seen with a unit of the **'Division Hermann Göring'** in Italy, summer of 1943.

Close-up view of the **Schachtellaufwerk** (staggered running gear). The staggered, rubber-tired, pressed steel road wheels ran on the lubricated tracks. The very complicated tracks of all German half-track vehicles required constant maintenance, however performed excellently if the necessary maintenance level was kept up.

78. Sturmdivision

In Russia as well as in Africa, the 8t prime mover served satisfactorily in many roles and under all conditions.

Pulling two Mercedes-Benz L 3000A 3t trucks, the **8t Zgkw.** is moving through the marshy terrain of Northern Russia.

Schwerer Zugkraftwagen 12t (Sd.Kfz. 8)

The late 20's and early 30's witnessed a close cooperation between the German **Reichswehr** and the Red Army. This unusual union was brought about by the Treaty of Versailles, putting a heavy ban on Germany's weapon development.

Many German military vehicles and weapons were tested in Russia. Some of these were also accepted by the Red Army, and orders were given to Germany's industry for the 9t prime mover designed and built by Daimler-Benz. The **Halbkettenzugwagen** 'ZD 5' was built and tested, but not accepted by the Soviets.

The Daimler-Benz 'DB s 7' entered troop service in 1934 to be replaced by the improved **Typ 'DB s 8'** of 1936. This vehicle remained in production for two years, when the Maybach HL 85 powered '**DB s 9**' left the production line in 1938. Having a crew of 13 men and a loading capacity of 1.6t, the 15t vehicle served primarily to pull heavy cannon. The final version of the **12t Zgkw. Series** appeared in late 1939 in the '**DB s 10**'.

Daimler-Benz, the Friedrich Krupp AG and Krauss-Maffei shared in the production of 4000 12t Zgkw. (**Sd.Kfz. 8**). A small number of vehicles were also built by Skoda, Prag.

Close-up view of the driver's cab and driving sprocket of a 12t 'DB 10'.

Technical Data

Producer . . . . Daimler-Benz
Crew . . . . 11 men
Weight . . . . 12.7 t
Dimensions .Length: 735 cm
                                          Height: 275 cm
                                          Width: 250 cm
Loading Capacity . . . . 2 t
Pulling Capacity . . . . 14 t
Motor . . . . 1 x 12 cyl. Maybach HL 85 TUKRM (gasoline)
                                          165 P.S. at 2500 r.p.m.
Speed . . . . .50 km/hr
Fuel Capacity. . . . . 250 liters (appr. 65 U.S. gal.)
Fuel Consumption . . . . .Road 100 liters, cross-country 220 liters / 100 km.
Range . . . . Road 250 km, cross-country 110 km.

The 12t **Zgkw. (Sd.Kfz. 8)** during driving practice of a future prime mover driver. The vehicle was powered by a 12 cylinder Maybach gasoline engine with 185 h.p.

A 12t prime mover with the 8.8 cm **Flak 36.** Camouflaged in **Wehrmacht** sand with brown-green mottle, with **Luftwaffe** license plate and black canvas top, this **Sd.Kfz. 8** would make an interesting plastic model kit and a necessary addition to a complete armor unit.

Schwerer Zugkraftwagen 18t (Sd.Kfz. 9)

The largest of the **Wehrmachtschlepper** was the **18t s.Zgkw. FAMO 'F3'** (**Sd.Kfz. 9**).

It took as many as three of the big 18t **Famo** prime movers to move a disabled 'Panther' or 'Tiger I'. The Tiger II **'Königstiger'**, with its 75t weight, just couldn't be rescued.

Development of the gigantic prime mover weighing over 15t was solely executed by the Fahrzeug and Motorenbau GmbH 'FAMO' Breslau, Oberschlesien. Two main types of the **s.Zgkw.** were delivered to the German Army and were intended for towing tank transport trailers up to 35t.

Development of the **Typ 'FM gr 1'** was concluded in 1936 to be followed by the improved **'FZ'** two years later. Powered by a 250 P.S. Maybach engine, the vehicle had a separate crew compartment for 8 men and a loading capacity of 2.8t. The final version, of which over 2000 were built until the end of 1944, appeared in 1939. The **s.Zgkw. 18t Typ F3** was powered by a 12 cylinder 250 P.S. Maybach engine and developed a towing capacity of 18,000 kg (18t). The vehicles performed well under all weather conditions and their immense silhouette was a common sight on all Fronts during the Second World War.

Technical Data

Producer	FAMO, Breslau, Warschau, Poland
Crew	8 men
Weight	15 t
Dimensions:	
Length	825 cm
Height	285 cm
Width	260 cm
Loading Capacity	2.8 t
Pulling Capacity	18 t
Motor	1 x 12 cyl. Maybach HL 108 TUKRM 250 P.S. at 2600 r.p.m.
Transmission	8 forward, 2 reverse
Speed	50 km/h
Fuel Capacity	290 liters (appr. 75 U.S. gal.)
Fuel Consumption:	
Road	120 ltr/100 km
Cross-Country	270 ltr/100 km
Range:	
Road	240 km
Cross-Country	100 km

Built exclusively by Famo Breslau and Warsaw, the 18t vehicle was primarily used for retrieving disabled tanks.

The tank tracks to the left indicate that the **Famos** are retrieving a 'Panther'.

The soldiers are dwarfed by the size of this prime mover.

As this picture indicates, it takes three **18t s.Zgkw.** to retrieve a disabled 60t Tiger I, barely visible through the dust.

Schwerer Wehrmacht-Schlepper (s.W.S.)

Technical Data

Crew . . . . .2 men	Motor . . . . 6 cyl. Maybach HL 42 TRKMS (gasoline)
Weight . . . . .9.5 t	100 P.S. at 3000 r.p.m.
Dimensions:	Transmission . . . . 4 forward, 1 reverse
Length . . . . 667 cm	Speed . . . . 28 km/h road
Height .285 cm	Fuel Capacity . . . . 240 liters
Width .250 cm	Fuel Consumption . . . . Road 80 ltr/100 km, Cross-Country 160 ltr/100 km
Loading Capacity . . . . 4 t	Range . . . . Road 300 km, Cross-Country 150 km
Pulling Capacity . . . . 8 t	